POLAR REGIONS

The North Pole is at the top of planet Earth. It is located in the Arctic Ocean. The water at the North Pole is almost always covered with ice.

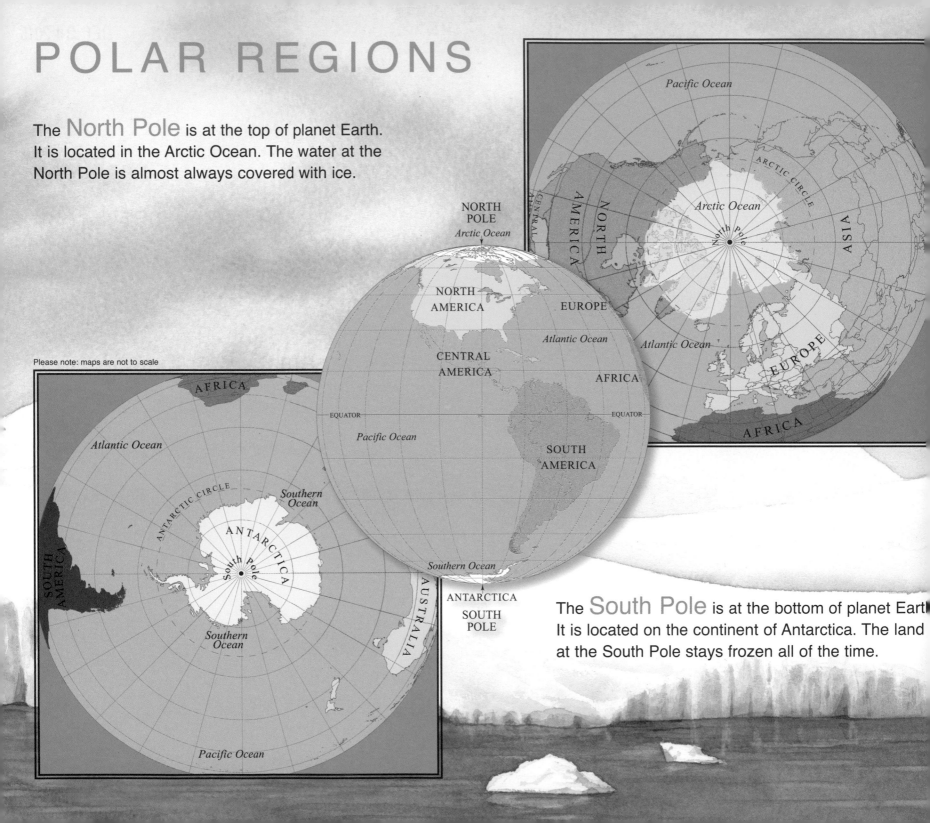

Please note: maps are not to scale

The South Pole is at the bottom of planet Earth. It is located on the continent of Antarctica. The land at the South Pole stays frozen all of the time.

ABOUT HABITATS

Polar Regions

To the One who created polar regions.
—*Genesis* 1:9–10

Ω

Published by
PEACHTREE PUBLISHERS
1700 Chattahoochee Avenue
Atlanta, Georgia 30318-2112
www.peachtree-online.com

Text © 2015 by Cathryn P. Sill
Illustrations © 2015 by John C. Sill

Illustrations created in watercolor on archival quality 100% rag watercolor paper.
Text and titles set in Novarese from Adobe.

Printed in April 2015 by Imago in Singapore
10 9 8 7 6 5 4 3 2 1
First Edition

Library of Congress Cataloging-in-Publication Data

Sill, Cathryn P., 1953- author.
  About habitats : polar regions / Cathryn Sill ; illustrated by John Sill.
     pages cm. — (About habitats)
  Includes bibliographical references.
  ISBN 978-1-56145-832-5
  1. Ecology—Polar regions—Juvenile literature. 2. Animals—Polar regions—Juvenile
literature. 3. Polar regions—Juvenile literature. I. Sill, John, illustrator. II. Title. III.
Title: Polar regions. IV. Series: Sill, Cathryn P., 1953- About habitats.
  QH84.1.S55 2015
  577.0911—dc23
                              2015002401

Polar Regions

Written by **Cathryn Sill**   Illustrated by **John Sill**

PEACHTREE
ATLANTA

Polar regions are the cold, windy places around the world's North and South Poles.

The area at the North Pole is the Arctic. It is made up of frozen ocean with land all around.

The area at the South Pole is called the Antarctic. It is made up of a huge area of frozen land with ocean all around.

Some parts of polar regions are covered
with ice all year long.

PLATE 4
ANTARCTIC

During winter, the sun never rises
and the days are long and cold.

In summer, the sun shines all day and night and the days are a little warmer.

PLATE 6
ARCTIC, ANTARCTIC

Orca

The ice melts in some places during the long, sunny days.

Plants are able to live in these warmer parts of polar regions.

The plants in polar regions grow close to the ground, where they are protected from the cold wind.

Animals live in different parts
of polar regions.

a.

b.

c.

d.

They have special ways to survive
the cold temperatures.

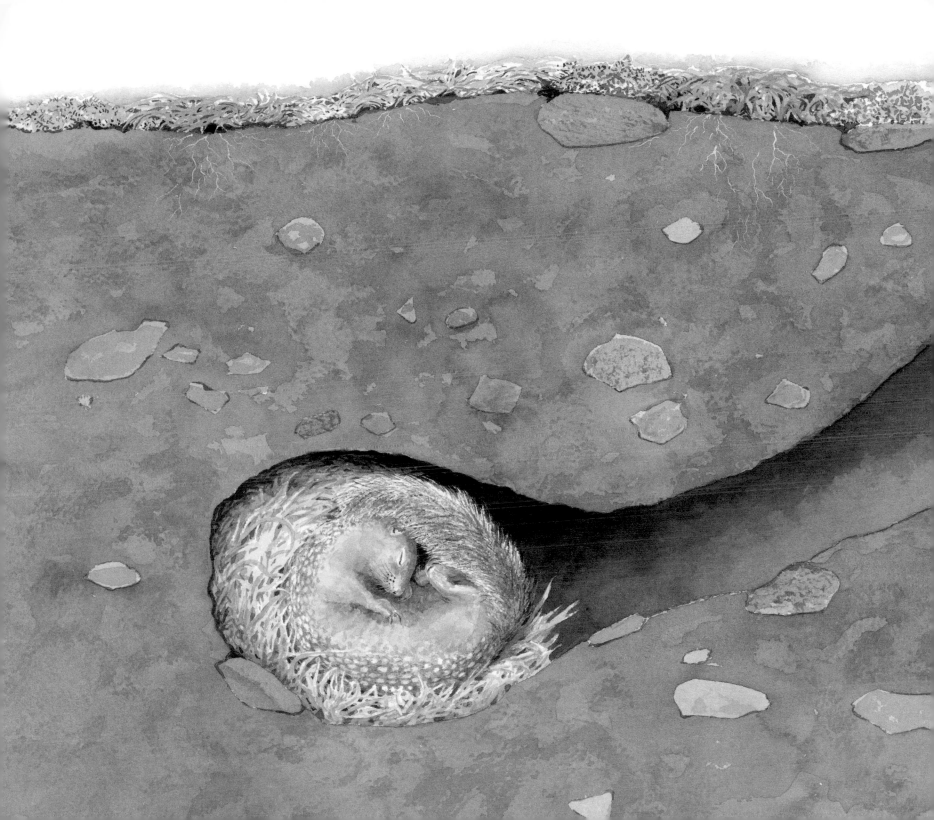

Most polar animals live in the ocean,
where it is warmer.

PLATE 12
ANTARCTIC

Sea Anemone
Sea Spider
Sea Star

Many have a thick layer of fat called blubber.

Some fish in polar regions have a special kind of blood that keeps them from freezing.

Animals that live on land have thick fur or
warm feathers to protect them from the cold.

Some live in dens or tunnels under the snow.

Others move to warmer places during winter.

PLATE 17
ARCTIC, ANTARCTIC

Arctic Tern

Polar regions are important places
that need to be protected.

POLAR REGIONS

Afterword

PLATE 1

Polar regions—the Arctic and the Antarctic—are located at the top and bottom of the world. Though alike in many ways, the two regions have many differences, including the types of animals living in each. Penguins live only in the Southern Hemisphere. Adélie Penguins are common along the Antarctic coast.

PLATE 2

Much of the Arctic is covered with floating sea ice. At the North Pole, the ocean stays frozen all the time. The continents of North America, Europe, and Asia surround the Arctic. Narwhals are able to swim and hunt under the pack ice, coming up to cracks and holes to breathe. The males have a tooth growing through their skin that forms a long tusk. Narwhals live year-round in the Arctic.

PLATE 3

The Antarctic polar region is located on the continent called Antarctica. Some areas in Antarctica get so little snow they are considered deserts. Storms with powerful winds are common in this polar region. Weddell Seals spend much time below the Antarctic pack ice. They use their strong teeth to keep their breathing holes in the ice from freezing over. Weddell Seals raise their babies further south than any other mammal.

PLATE 4

Both poles are covered with ice caps that are always frozen. Ocean temperatures in polar regions are warmer than land. Because so much of the Antarctic is land, it is colder than the Arctic. The sea ice in the Arctic can be 7 to 10 feet (2 to 3 meters) thick in winter. In the Antarctic, the ice is over 15,000 feet (4,572 meters) thick in some places. There are mountains, valleys, and lakes under the Antarctic ice.

PLATE 5

Polar regions are the coldest places on Earth. Weather conditions are so harsh that very few people live there. The lowest temperature ever recorded on Earth's surface (-129.5°F or -89.2°C) was in Antarctica. Sometimes the Antarctic winter skies are lit by the aurora australis (southern lights). Male Emperor Penguins spend long cold winters on the Antarctic ice taking care of their eggs and chicks During this time, the mothers are at sea hunting for food.

PLATE 6

When it is summer at one pole, the other pole is having winter. In summer the pole is closer to the sun and in winter it is farther away from the sun. In polar regions, even the summer temperatures are cool. They never average over 50°F (10°c) in midsummer. Orcas live in the oceans at both polar regions. Even though they are sometimes called "Killer Whales," Orcas are dolphins. They are the largest member of the dolphin family.

PLATE 7

Snow and ice disappear from the Arctic tundra in summer, and a variety of plants can grow there. During this season many animals are able to find food and a safe place to raise their young. Muskoxen are plant eaters that live on the tundra all year. In winter they dig through the snow with their sharp hooves to find mosses, roots, and lichens to eat. Meat eaters like Arctic Wolves hunt Muskoxen and other animals.

PLATE 8

Most of Antarctica is under ice all the time. No trees or shrubs grow there. Antarctic Hair Grass and Antarctic Pearlwort are the only two flowering plants that are able to live in Antarctica. Antarctic Hair Grass is found on the Antarctic Peninsula, where temperatures are warmer and some of the ice melts in summer. It grows near the coast, where it is sometimes trampled and destroyed by Antarctic Fur Seals.

PLATE 9

The Arctic tundra is covered with permafrost. Only the top layer of soil thaws each summer. Because the ground underneath stays frozen, big plants with large root systems are not able to grow. The plants often grow in clumps, and this helps them stay warm. Some of them are covered with fuzzy hairs that protect them from the cold. American Golden Plovers build nests and raise their young on the North American Arctic tundra.

PLATE 10

Snow Petrels nest on inland cliffs in Antarctica. Walruses often rest on ice floes in the Arctic. Chinstrap Penguins raise their babies on rocky coasts in the Antarctic region. Each summer, Caribou migrate to the Arctic tundra, where they eat the grasses and other plants that grow there.

PLATE 11

Because food is so hard to find, not many land animals spend winters in polar regions. Arctic Ground Squirrels hibernate for about seven months each year. They spend the warmer months eating and getting fat enough to survive the long hibernation. Their food includes plant parts such as blades of grass, stems, leaves, berries, and seeds. They also eat mushrooms, insects, bird eggs, and carrion. Arctic Ground Squirrels live in the Arctic tundra in North America and eastern Russia.

PLATE 12

Even though water in polar oceans is very cold, it is warmer than the land. Polar oceans swarm with tiny plants and animals that are food for larger animals. The ocean floor around Antarctica is home to many creatures, including sea anemones, sea stars, and sea spiders.

PLATE 13

A thick layer of blubber is located just under the skin of most ocean mammals. It acts like a heavy coat to keep the animals warm in cold water. Southern Elephant Seals are the largest seals. They get their name from their trunk-like noses. They have their babies on land but spend the winters in the cold ocean near the Antarctic pack ice.

PLATE 14

The ocean temperature gets down to 28°F (-2°C) in places around Antarctica. This is cold enough to freeze the blood of most fishes. Many Antarctic fish, including icefish, produce a kind of antifreeze that keeps them from freezing in icy water. Because icefish have no red blood cells, their blood is nearly clear. Blackfin Icefish hunt for small fish and krill on the ocean bottom in the Antarctic.

PLATE 15

The fur or feathers of some animals that live in polar regions year-round turn white in winter. When the snow cover melts in summer their fur and feathers are dark. This provides camouflage for the animals during both seasons. Arctic Foxes have one of the warmest coats of any mammal. Special feathers on the legs and feet of Rock Ptarmigans help them stay warm. Arctic Foxes and Rock Ptarmigans live in the Arctic.

PLATE 16

Like a warm blanket, snow helps protect animals from strong winds and cold temperatures. In winter, Northern Collared Lemmings grow large claws on their front feet that help them dig tunnels. They stay active all winter eating bark, buds, and twigs found under the snow. Northern Collared Lemmings live in the Arctic tundra in North America and Greenland.

PLATE 17

As the weather gets colder, it gets harder for some polar animals to find food. Arctic Terns raise their young in the Arctic during the summer, when they can find plenty of food such as fish, crustaceans, and insects. When winter comes to the Arctic, it is summer in the Antarctic. The terns travel south to spend the rest of the year there. Arctic Terns have one of the longest migrations of any animal.

PLATE 18

Polar regions are threatened by overfishing, whaling, pollution, tourism, and climate change. Even small changes in the environment can make survival much harder for polar animals and plants. Polar Bears are the largest predator in the Arctic. They spend most of their time on the sea ice, hunting for seals. Melting of the ice pack due to warmer temperatures is causing concern for the future of Polar Bears.

GLOSSARY

BIOME—an area such as a forest or wetland that shares the same types of plants and animals

ECOSYSTEM—a community of living things and their environment

HABITAT—the place where animals and plants live

camouflage—colors or patterns on an animal that help it hide

carrion—dead and decaying flesh

continent—one of seven main masses of land on the earth

ice floe—a piece of floating ice

krill—small shrimplike crustaceans that live in the ocean

pack ice—a large area of floating ice made up of smaller pieces that have been squeezed together

permafrost—a layer of soil that is always frozen

predator—an animal that lives by hunting and eating other animals

BIBLIOGRAPHY

BOOKS

BIODIVERSITY OF POLAR REGIONS by Greg Pyers (Marshall Cavendish)

DISCOVER SCIENCE: POLAR LANDS by Margaret Hynes (Kingfisher)

EARTH MATTERS: AN ENCYCLOPEDIA OF ECOLOGY edited by David Rothschild (DK Publishing)

I WONDER WHY PENGUINS CAN'T FLY: AND OTHER QUESTIONS ABOUT POLAR LANDS by Pat Jacobs (Kingfisher)

WEBSITES

http://worldwildlife.org/habitats/polar-regions

http://www.mbgnet.net/

http://www.thewildclassroom.com/biomes/index.html

ABOUT... SERIES

ISBN 978-1-56145-234-7 HC
ISBN 978-1-56145-312-2 PB

ISBN 978-1-56145-038-1 HC
ISBN 978-1-56145-364-1 PB

ISBN 978-1-56145-688-8 HC
ISBN 978-1-56145-699-4 PB

ISBN 978-1-56145-301-6 HC
ISBN 978-1-56145-405-1 PB

ISBN 978-1-56145-256-9 HC
ISBN 978-1-56145-335-1 PB

ISBN 978-1-56145-588-1 HC
ISBN 978-1-56145-837-0 PB

ISBN 978-1-56145-881-3 HC
ISBN 978-1-56145-882-0 PB

ISBN 978-1-56145-757-1 HC
ISBN 978-1-56145-758-8 PB

ISBN 978-1-56145-358-0 HC
ISBN 978-1-56145-407-5 PB

ISBN 978-1-56145-331-3 HC
ISBN 978-1-56145-406-8 PB

ISBN 978-1-56145-795-3 HC

ISBN 978-1-56145-743-4 HC
ISBN 978-1-56145-741-0 PB

ISBN 978-1-56145-536-2 HC
ISBN 978-1-56145-811-0 PB

ISBN 978-1-56145-183-8 HC
ISBN 978-1-56145-233-0 PB

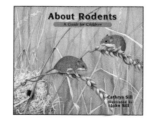

ISBN 978-1-56145-454-9 HC

**ALSO AVAILABLE
IN BILINGUAL EDITION**

- About Birds / Sobre los pájaros
  ISBN 978-1-56145-783-0 PB
- About Mammals / Sobre los mamíferos
  ISBN 978-1-56145-800-4 PB
- About Insects / Sobre los insectos
  ISBN 978-1-56145-883-7 PB

ABOUT HABITATS SERIES

ISBN 978-1-56145-641-3 HC
ISBN 978-1-56145-636-9 PB

ISBN 978-1-56145-734-2 HC

ISBN 978-1-56145-559-1 HC

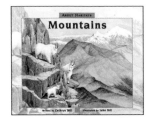

ISBN 978-1-56145-469-3 HC
ISBN 978-1-56145-731-1 PB

ISBN 978-1-56145-618-5 HC

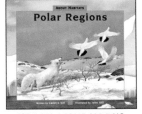

ISBN 978-1-56145-832-5 HC

ISBN 978-1-56145-432-7 HC
ISBN 978-1-56145-689-5 PB

THE SILLS

CATHRYN AND JOHN SILL are the dynamic team who created the *About…* series as well as the *About Habitats* series. Their books have garnered praise from educators and have won a variety of awards, including Bank Street Best Books, CCBC Choices, NSTA/CBC Outstanding Science Trade Books for Students K–12, Orbis Pictus Recommended, and *Science Books and Films* Best Books of the Year. Cathryn, a graduate of Western Carolina State University, taught early elementary school classes for thirty years. John holds a BS in wildlife biology from North Carolina State University. Combining his artistic skill and knowledge of wildlife, he has achieved an impressive reputation as a wildlife artist. The Sills live in Franklin, North Carolina.

PHOTO BY ANDREW SPENCER